I0181719

Poetry Time

An Inspirational Collection of Acrostic and Traditional Poems

SHEILA EISMANN

Volume One
Desert Sage Press
www.desertsagepress.com

Sheila Eismann

Published by Desert Sage Press
www.desertsagepress.com

Printed and bound in the United States of America.

Cover graphic image: 81520398 @ www.fotolia.com
Used by permission. All rights reserved.

ISBN: 978-0-9897133-5-1
Library of Congress Control Number: 2016908285

Poetry Time

An Inspirational Collection of Acrostic and Traditional Poems

Sheila Eismann

DEDICATION

This book is dedicated to poetry and prose readers all around the globe. May the challenging, encouraging, inspiring, and uplifting words on the pages within cause your souls and spirits to soar to new heights!

BOOKS BY SHEILA EISMANN

A STORMY YEAR

A WOMAN OF SUBSTANCE

HEART TO HEART FROM GOD'S WORD

LOVE, THE TIE THAT BINDS

JANTZI'S JOKERS

POETRY TIME – VOLUME ONE

RECOGNIZE YOUR CIRCLES

STIRRINGS OF THE SPIRIT

STRAIGHT FROM THE HORSE'S TROUGH

THE CHRISTMAS TIN

CONTENTS

Forever Friends

Throughout your life
    people will come and go,
Some will be real
    while others are just show.

Be careful in whose heart
    you deposit your dreams,
For in a mere moment
    they can be made into schemes.

There will be times
    to keep things close to your vest,
Lest your supposed friends
    take from you your best.

Learn to get wisdom
    and to walk with the wise,
Chances are then
    that you'll not be led to your demise.

Suddenly if you are blessed
    with an abundance of wealth,
Learn how to operate
    in a mode of stealth.

Fame, fortune or affluence
    seem to attract like flies,
Those whose real motives
    are cheating and lies.

A lot of humanity
    is not bent on evil or sin,
They're trying to make this world
    a better place if they can.

If you've been blessed
    with forever friends,
You have been given something
    that never ends.

Love Is

Love is like a flower
     that never fades away.
It blooms forth ever so brightly
     and does not close at the end of day.

Love is like a fragrant aroma
     that lingers in the air.
Its scent grows even stronger
     when matched up with a pair.

Love is like a delicious dessert
     piled high with whipping cream.
It covers over a multitude of sins
     and helps you live your dream.

Love is that touch of a tender hand
     that signals you are special.
It's quite often extended
     just when your need is crucial.

Love is the song that plays
     upon the tender strings of your heart.

Its melody is the shield
    that will protect you from the fiery dart.

So reach out and
    See
    Smell
    Taste
    Touch
    And listen to love today!

You will be glad you did,
    and it will keep you from fading away.

God Sent Me an Angel Today

You must have been listening
      during your prayer time today,
Because I know that Almighty God
      surely sent you my way.

Words are inadequate to express
      my sincere appreciation and thanks,
As I have felt all day long that
      I was withdrawing from Heaven's Banks.

You are truly one of a kind
      with your servant's mind and heart,
Knowing just the right thing to do
      from the very start.

Please know what a blessing you are
      to me and my clan,
It's comforting to know
      that God always has a plan.

Sheila Eismann

For He works through people
    in the most mysterious of ways,

So I am asking God in heaven
    to bless you all of your days.

Thank you with all of my heart ~ ~ ~

Memories

Do you have lots of memories
    or just a mere few?
And are they like treasures
    that you take out and view?

Where are the dark ones
    you would like to forget?
Have you buried them forever
    or are you digging them up still yet?

Do yourself a favor
    and retain only the best,
For if you do this
    you can live your life with zest!

If others continue to parade
    your less than favorite one,
Tell them to stop it
    as this they should not have done.

The heart and mind
    are meant to be complete,

And this will never be
    as long as there is a bad repeat.

Resolve to be kind to yourself
    As you fill your memory bank,
With the crème de la crème ones
    and not those that stank.

Help someone else
    along their memory journey,
Taking what you have learned,
    and deliver it with honey.

Each of us has many choices
    as life unfolds each day.
I choose to fill my recollection storehouse
    in just the right way!

Help Is On The Way

The last time I checked
    I had made a great discovery,
If you give it some thought
    it may not be such a mystery.

Alas, the final outcome was
    such a pleasant surprise,
I've been telling my friends
    just to get a rise.

My current non-existent, non-benefit payroll
    consists of the following alphabetical lineup:

    Anna the Administrator
    Audrey the Author
    Betty the Baker
    Bobbie the Bookkeeper
    Constance the Cook
    Hannah the Housekeeper
    Inez the Ironess

Linda the Laundress
Natalie the Notary
Quaylene the QuickBooker
Savannah the Secretary
Tammy the Tax Preparer
Tonya the Taxi Driver
Yvette the Yard Worker

Each of the aforementioned
    is so efficient and kind,
If they stay on schedule
    I'm never left in a bind.

So live your life on the lighter side,
    and write out your list today.
You'll make some great progress
    even if it's without pay!

Greater Than

God Is Greater Than

Any betrayal

Any death

Any disappointment

Any disenfranchisement

Any loss

Any pain

Any sacrifice

Choose to place your hand in His,

    and walk with Him every day.

He is a trusted guide and Father,

    Who will never lead you astray.

Sheila Eismann

Thankful

The fruit of our lips giving thanks,
Heard by many far and wide,
Affirms Your greatness and power,
Nurturing those who choose to abide.
Kindness flows from Your throne,
Faithfulness right behind,
Unmerited favor granted here and there,
Lessens our daily grind.

Sheila Eismann

Let's Take Time To Celebrate

Remembering back to when
    we first said, "I do",
I knew that I had found
    just the perfect you.

Our love has been tested
    time and time again,
But God forged us together
    from when we first began.

True love has a way
    of binding hearts and minds,
It's the perfect solution
    for the foxes that spoil the vines.

Let's take time to celebrate
    the life we've made together,
Making memories fresh and new
    adding to the splendor.

Sheila Eismann

Happy Anniversary with all of my love ~ ~ ~

Now and forever.

Harvest

Help me to see the lost,
As I travel through this day.
Ready my heart to help,
Various people still at bay.
Everyone can use a helping hand,
Some will choose Your way.
Tomorrow may be too late!

Sheila Eismann

A Mere Mortal

Heavenly Father, I am but a mere mortal,
    and do not comprehend Your ways.
As I continue in my walk with You,
    I simply marvel at the Ancient of Days.

Only You know the end from the beginning,
    so help me to trust as You guide my steps.
When the storms of life come blowing through,
    please keep me from plunging into the depths.

You will always be there for me
    through all of the circumstances of life;
Whether filled with joy, gladness, and victory,
    or tragedy, discouragement, and strife.

I thank You for all that You have done for me,
    and the gifts You have bestowed from above;
Chief among these are Your beloved Son Jesus,
    along with Your constant abiding love.

My gifts to You are my heart and my will,
    coupled with a desire to do what is right.
For then one day I shall prayerfully become
    a vessel of honor in my Master's sight.

Trials

Trials seem to be guaranteed,

Regardless of where we abound.

Inside every one of them,

Arises a God Who is very sound.

Let us continue to rejoice,

So in the end our faith may be found.

Sheila Eismann

Forgiveness

Oh, what a priceless gift
    my Savior gave to me,
When He died on that old rugged cross
    for all of the world to see.

He shed His royal innocent blood
    with much pain and agony,
But wavered not from showing
    obedience so faithfully.

I have now come to realize
    how unworthy I must be,
To receive such a pardon
    for all of my iniquity.

But my Master, Savior, and friend
    spoke so very quietly,
"Come, my dear child, and take this gift
    which I offer so willingly."

Sheila Eismann

"After you have received and can
     appreciate it so thoroughly,
Proclaim my gift of forgiveness
     and set someone else free."

Purified by His Flame

The temperature of His flame increases
    through the storms and tests of life,
Revealing the impurities present
    along with the remaining blight.

"'Tis unfair!" we may be tempted to shout
    until we pause to ask,
"Just what is this unpleasant
    heat all about?"

Jesus is returning soon for His pure bride
    without blemish, wrinkle or spot.
She needs to get herself ready
    because she's already been bought.

The price was drastically paid
    some 2,000 years ago,
When Jesus shed His precious blood
    as others watched it flow.

Sheila Eismann

This act of obedience was completed
     for the entire human race,
God does not want you to perish,
     but to end up in the correct place.

If you hear God's voice today
     turn the dial to *high*,
Answer quickly with a "yes"
     and don't let out a sigh.

We can cast our cares upon Him
     as we know He cares for us.
What a huge relief this is,
     so we don't have to fuss.

The keeper of the flame
     knows just the exact degree,
He controls the temperature
     when you need to bow your knee.

So lean into the flame that appears,
     don't shrink back or resist.
Allow the refiner's fire
     to ready you for His visit.

Strength & Courage

Summon your strength
To wage the battles you need to fight.
Resolve to use wisdom
Engaging with all of your might.
Never give up
Go the distance and then some.
Tell yourself you can do it
Hold on 'til you've won.

&

Count the cost of your dreams
Outrageous as they may appear.
Understanding that you must
Rise above all your fear.
Add some courage to the mix
Generating excitement to boot
Encourage others to follow suit.

Sheila Eismann

Eternity

Father God, as I quietly ponder eternity
    which You established long ago,
Help me not to be overcome by the future
    of which I do not know.

Each and every one of Your special creations
    has had equal chance and grace,
To accept Your beloved Son Jesus
    and secure their future place.

When You usher in Your glorious
    new heaven and new earth,
One cannot help but dream and wonder
    what will be wrought by this new birth.

Well, enough of this pondering I say,
    I will just wait for the trumpet call.
I can hardly wait to see my Jesus
    riding on His steed so tall.

Following these spectacular events

Sheila Eismann

Following these spectacular events
     I will know the answers forever.
For it is then that I will meet with you
     and we will spend eternity together.

Someday

Someday I'll find the time
    to do the things I want to do.
I'll venture into the attic
    and find the recipe for that roux.

The ancestral trees on both sides
    continue to call my name,
Reminding me ever so gently
    that they're nowhere near the same.

Aunt Allene's heirloom quilt
    must be removed from its display rack,
As it beckons me to follow
    the nine-patch pattern in the stack.

Audrey insists her roma tomatoes
    produce the finest salsa yet,
To which one must add cilantro
    and jalapenos for extra zest!

Sheila Eismann

Foreign lands seem so intriguing
    and not just via the news.
The globe is meant to be traveled
    while one can still pick and choose.

So many books with so little time
    carry me to enchanting places.
Rella's brown velour couch or chair
    vie for the comfortable spaces.

Orion and the Big Dipper glisten
    as diamonds in the night sky.
Shall I purchase a nice telescope
    to watch them by and by?

Alas, yesterday is history and
    tomorrow may not be.
If I continue to wait for someday
    my desires I will never see.

Bless

Bless you Lord
Light of the world
Emmanuel
Savior of my soul
So good to me!

Sheila Eismann

A Child of God

I am a child of God,
    an example of His diversity.
I am one of His creations
    in all of my complexity.

He knit me together inside my mother's womb,
    each stitch so carefully made.
He labored in the dark
    to achieve His excellent grade.

There is no one else like me
    in His vast universe.
I am a one-of-a-kind person
    with my own special song and verse.

You, too are a child of God,
    a one-of-a-kind creation.
If you searched the world over,
    you would never find a duplication.

God makes no mistakes
    with anything He creates.
So stand strong in your individuality,
    and draw upon His glory and grace.

Take Time

Take time during each day
    to pause and reflect,
Give thanks for your blessings
    even if they aren't perfect.

Take time to tell those you love
    how much they mean to you.
There may come a day
    when they are no longer in view.

Take time to pen a letter or note
    just to say thanks or a mere hello.
You just might be the bright spot
    that helps a life to glow.

Take time to perform
    a good deed or two,
Lessen someone else's burden,
    so they won't have to cry boo-hoo.

Sheila Eismann

Take time to watch a sunset
     with its tapestry aflame,
Let it warm your heart and spirit
     and readjust your game.

Take time to plan your work
     and to work your plan,
This will save you hours and weeks
     down the road a span.

Take time to honor those in your life
     even if they don't deserve it now.
For surely you will have shown them a better way,
     and then you can take a bow.

Take time for yourself above all else
     to nurture your own life and spirit.
For if you will do this
     then you will greatly benefit.

Promises

Pressing into You Sweet Jesus,
Rejoicing in the cross.
Overcoming with Your power,
Making disciples of those who are lost.
Inwardly feeling your presence,
Satisfied at the end of each day.
Endeavoring to be more Christ-like,
Sharing Your love along the way.

Sheila Eismann

Captivity

I once resided in captivity
    until I accepted Jesus as my Lord.
Then the shackles started falling off
    as I began to walk a new road.

Does Satan have your soul bound
    to his eternal hell?
Does he have you in bondage
    or under his awful spell?

I declare to you this very day,
    "Rise up in strength and do not cower!"
Decide from this moment on
    that Satan will no longer have power.

Proceed to confess with your mouth
    that Jesus Christ is Lord,
And believe in your heart
    that God raised Him from the dead.

At that very moment
    you shall inherit salvation.
And the angels in heaven
    wll begin their celebration!

Tears In A Bottle

Tears here, tears there,
    tears seem to be everywhere.
Flowing ever so freely,
    at times quite hard to bear.

It seems each one is counted
    by the angels of God above.
As they mark them in His book
    with precision, care, and love.

God is the tear tracker
    placing every one is His bottle,
Surely there would be no way
    to measure or build His model.

There will come a day
    when every tear will be wiped away.
Gone will be the pain and sorrow
    that have held us in sway.

Until the time has come
    for God to call you home,
There's never really a minute
    when you need to feel alone.

If your name has been recorded
    in the Lamb's Book of Life,
Pay no attention to daily worries,
    wars, rumors or strife.

So when you shed your next tear
    be sure not to think,
That it won't be counted and collected
    before you can blink!

Labor

Looking unto You, Jesus,
Awaiting Your trumpet call.
Busy in Your kingdom,
Owning no worries at all.
Resting in Your love.

Sheila Eismann

The Victor's Crown

Jesus is our reigning King
    Who wears the victor's crown.
Though many have waged war against Him
    and tried to bring Him down.

The enemy of our souls
    or Lucifer by name,
Challenged Jesus Christ one day
    and tried to bring Him shame.

But Satan, that serpent of old,
    was no match for God's only Son,
Because Jesus defeated him on the cross
    in the battle of one-on-one.

King Jesus continues to rule
    from His lofty heavenly domain.
All principalities and powers
    must bow at the mention of His name.

Would you like to wear a victor's crown
    when your life on earth has expired?
Choose Jesus Christ as your personal Savior
    and He will fulfill that great desire.

Justified

Journeys can be long and hard,
Under duress along the way.
Storms appear out of nowhere,
Treasures are kept at bay.
Island retreats are hard to find,
Freedoms seem to sway.
In Jesus I have placed my trust,
Eternity is where I will stay.
Dancing with my Savior each and every day!

Sheila Eismann

The Real One

There is one single name
    that has brought controversy and strife,
Yet to those who have believed in Him
    it has brought everlasting life.

Whoever would have thought
    that the life of a Jewish carpenter
Would turn the world upside down
    through His ministry, proclamations and character?

Jesus, the King, possesses many names
    each with its own distinct nature.
But the important one for you to acquire
    is that of personal Lord and Savior.

Many have claimed to be the Christ,
    but scripture states there is only one.
The real Jesus is both Almighty God
    and His precious begotten Son.

Sheila Eismann

If the above verses do not ring true
    to what you have learned in the past,
Delve into God's Holy Word,
    and ascertain the truth at last.

Grace

God's unmerited favor

Ready for those who choose His Son.

Available around the clock

Consideration for everyone

Enter into His salvation.

Sheila Eismann

Generations

When my first generation began
    I have no clue,
Dwelling upon it now and then
    I certainly wish I knew.

Who married who
    and how did they become acquainted?
Was it love at first sight
    or a romance quite belated?

Where did they live
    and how did they get to the states?
Was it by air, land, or sea
    as they awaited their fates?

Were their life spans
    lengthy or short?
How many of their dreams
    did they have to abort?

Sheila Eismann

Occupations, interests, and hobbies
        were probably quite varied.
If they were listed on a wall
        it probably couldn't be carried.

God ultimately decided
        in which clan to place me.
My children and I would become
        part of my family tree.
Since He makes no mistakes,
        I'm exactly where I need to be.

'Tis The Reason For The Season

In the hustle and bustle of the season,
    have you stopped to consider the reason?

Why do we toil so everything will be first rate,
    waiting until December 25th just to celebrate?

Is your heart stirred by the good food,
    tree or gifts,
The music, cards, and parties,
    or the opening of ski-lifts?

Do you long to meet with family and friends
    that you all love so dearly,
To reminisce of times long ago
    that you still remember clearly?

Perhaps the passing of loved ones
    makes you feel lonely and sad,
It's hard to get through this time
    because you're just not very glad.

Sheila Eismann

Millennia ago, the prophet Isaiah foretold,
    that the virgin would bear a son,
Born in Bethlehem, and called Immanuel,
    His advent was a most humble one.

This baby boy, better known as Jesus,
    came to die on the cross for our sin.
Until we repent and accept Him as Savior,
    there's no way we will ever win.

Is Jesus knocking on the door of your heart
    or have you already let Him in?
Are you wearing your robe of righteousness
    or are you still living in your sin?

So take a moment, amidst your frantic pace
    to commune with the King of Kings.
For no one else can deliver joy and peace;
    none other gives the life He brings!

A Dozen Christmas Days

On the first day of Christmas
My true Lord gave to me:
Faith for any situation.

On the second day of Christmas
My true Lord gave to me:
Grace to stand in Him,
And faith for any situation.

On the third day of Christmas
My true Lord gave to me:
Ability to rejoice in sufferings,
Grace to stand in Him,
And faith for any situation.

On the fourth day of Christmas
My true Lord gave to me:
Plenty of perseverance,
Ability to rejoice in sufferings,
Grace to stand in Him,
And faith for any situation.

On the fifth day of Christmas
My true Lord gave to me:
Character built in the crucible!
Plenty of perseverance,
Ability to rejoice in sufferings,
Grace to stand in Him,
And faith for any situation.

On the sixth day of Christmas
My true Lord gave to me:
Hope as my soul's anchor,
Character built in the crucible!
Plenty of perseverance,
Ability to rejoice in sufferings,
Grace to stand in Him,
And faith for any situation.

On the seventh day of Christmas
My true Lord gave to me:
Abundant love when needed,
Hope as my soul's anchor,
Character built in the crucible!
Plenty of perseverance,
Ability to rejoice in sufferings,
Grace to stand in Him,
And faith for any situation.

On the eighth day of Christmas
My true Lord gave to me:
Joy to spread to others,
Abundant love when needed,
Hope as my soul's anchor,
Character built in the crucible!
Plenty of perseverance,
Ability to rejoice in sufferings,
Grace to stand in Him,
And faith for any situation.

On the ninth day of Christmas
My true Lord gave to me:
Truth to speak in love,
Joy to spread to others,
Abundant love when needed,
Hope as my soul's anchor,
Character built in the crucible!
Plenty of perseverance,
Ability to rejoice in sufferings,
Grace to stand in Him,
And faith for any situation.

On the tenth day of Christmas
My true Lord gave to me:
Understanding of His word,
Truth to speak in love,
Joy to spread to others,
Abundant love when needed,
Hope as my soul's anchor,
Character built in the crucible!
Plenty of perseverance,
Ability to rejoice in sufferings,
Grace to stand in Him,
And faith for any situation.

On the eleventh day of Christmas
My true Lord gave to me:
The gift of discernment,
Understanding of His word,
Truth to speak in love,
Joy to spread to others,
Abundant love when needed,
Hope as my soul's anchor,
Character built in the crucible!
Plenty of perseverance,
Ability to rejoice in sufferings,
Grace to stand in Him,
And faith for any situation.

Poetry Time

On the twelfth day of Christmas
My true Lord gave to me:
Peace that passes understanding,
The gift of discernment,
Understanding of His word,
Truth to speak in love,
Joy to spread to others,
Abundant love when needed,
Hope as my soul's anchor,
Character built in the crucible!
Plenty of perseverance,
Ability to rejoice in sufferings,
Grace to stand in Him,
And faith for any situation.

Sheila Eismann

ABOUT THE AUTHOR

Sheila Eismann, author and publisher of twelve books, is third in her lineage of five female writers and poets. She endeavors to enhance the lives of others through education and encouragement via penning her inspirational and fictional books. Eismann, co-founder of Idaho Creative Authors' Network (ICAN), speaks at Womens' and Writers' Conferences.

Please peruse Sheila's website www.sheilaeismann.com and sign up to receive her blog posts and newsletters. Send her an email at sheila@sheilaeismann.com to let her know which poem was your favorite in this book. Happy Reading!

Where to find Sheila Eismann online:

Email: sheila@sheilaeismann.com

Website: www.sheilaeismann.com

Facebook: www.facebook.com/sheila.eismann

Blog: www.sheilaeismann.com

LinkedIn: Sheila Eismann

Etsy Store: www.etsy.com/shop/BooksbySheilaEismann

AVAILABLE BOOKS TO READ FROM AUTHORS DANIEL AND SHEILA EISMANN which can be found at www.sheilaeismann.com & www.amazon.com:

Stirrings
of The Spirit

Sheila F Eismann

In this collection of true stories titled **Stirrings of The Spirit,** author Sheila F. Eismann invites you to walk with her family through several valleys en route to some mountain tops as they learned to rely on God in the most harrowing of circumstances.

RECOGNIZE
YOUR
CIRCLES

A Humorous Look
Into Life's
Relationships

Have you ever wondered why you were the last one to hear of THE big social event of the year? Well, wonder no longer after reading this e-book titled **Recognize Your Circles**! When volunteering for an organization years ago, author Sheila F. Eismann was introduced to the concept of "the circles of your life." Since the idea was so beneficial to her, she decided to share it with all of you.

Straight From the Horse's Trough
Gardening Help for
the Suburbanite and Urbanite

Sheila F. Eismann

Straight from the Horse's Trough is a humorous read to render assistance to the suburbanite or urbanite who desires to live a healthier lifestyle by growing his or her own food, but is faced with the challenge of a small space in which to do so. This e-book is chock full of how-to steps and includes pictures to remove guesswork from the project.

The Christmas Tin

By Sheila Faye Eismann & Ali Dawn Puez
Illustrated by Cathie Richardson

The Christmas Tin is a most delightful read for the young at heart anytime during the year. This endearing book is based upon a true story featuring the older of the two authors when she was a young girl and conveys the timeless message that "love truly is the best gift of all." Children will especially enjoy all of the colorful illustrations contained within this treasure and suggested hands on activities. Have some fun!

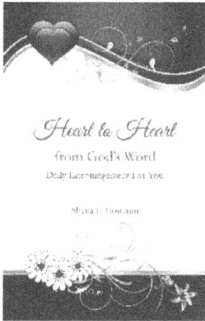

Everyone can use a little encouragement ~~ a dose of what is beneficial, ethical, and honorable. *Heart to Heart From God's Word* provides this for you. Penned with humor and wisdom, the daily tidbits are paired with Bible verses that convey life-changing principles which are designed for readers of all ages transcending cultures and continents. This devotional will challenge you to grow and fulfill your God-given destiny. It can also double as a prayer journal.

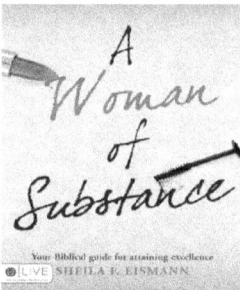

A Woman of Substance is a practical, interactive, and entertaining 12 week Bible study penned to help equip you to fulfill your God-given destiny and impact the culture for Jesus Christ at the same time. It can be used as a stand alone study or devotional and works well in a group setting, too. It is designed for women ages Junior High through adult.

FREEDOM IS
YOUR DESTINY!

Daniel T. Eismann

Freedom is Your Destiny! Vietnam Veteran, Dan Eismann, using combat experiences to illustrate spiritual truths, invites you to take a journey with him as he presents a rock-solid strategy for not only fighting your spiritual battles, but winning the all-important war. In the midst thereof, the most vital aspect is realizing you can experience freedom and become all that God has destined you to be!

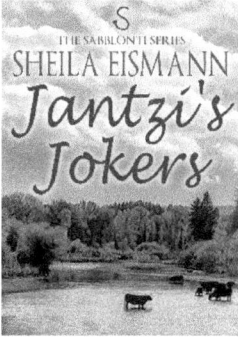

Western Fiction Book One of The Sabblonti Series, *Jantzi's Jokers*, features Jantzi Belle, matriarch of the Sabblonti family, who has worked for decades to keep her cattle empire intact. Life takes a drastic turn when she receives a late-night visitor. The brief disappearance of her Last Will and Testament could complicate matters between her daughters, Stormy and Sarita. Stormy and her husband, Chet Castins, are struggling to work through the loss of their three children. Against all odds, drifter Wyn Moreland makes a bold move when he decides that Sarita is his beauty to rescue. The county veterinarian, Dr. Ben Shaw, is also vying for her affections. Will Wyn emerge as the winner? Just prior to the dawn of the New Year, revelations come forth regarding forgery, cattle rustling, and land exploitation. Will the Sabblonti Empire survive, and more importantly, who will control its reins?

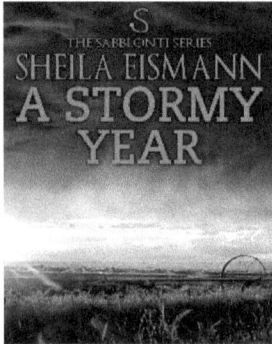

The Sabblonti Saga accelerates in Book Two of the Series, *A Stormy Year*. Riding her high horse after inheriting the family fortune, Stormy Castins is determined to reinvent herself following her husband's accident. Blinded by jealousy, ambition, and naivety, she hires Less and Meg Alotto to oversee her vast high desert mountain domain. While Stormy is away, the cattle herd ends up in disarray.

Amidst the hot dry season, romance is blooming on several fronts despite a major showdown during a mid-summer celebration. The pesky Black Raven continues to wreak havoc at the most inopportune times.

Unable to overcome the vengeance which strikes by way of a mysterious range fire combined with the dire deeds of a cagey couple, the Sabblonti Ranch is in shambles just as Stormy starts to regain her senses. Humility is the prescription needed to open her eyes in order to realize what's truly important in life. The sparks from a belated holiday rendevous set Chet and Stormy on their path to recovery.

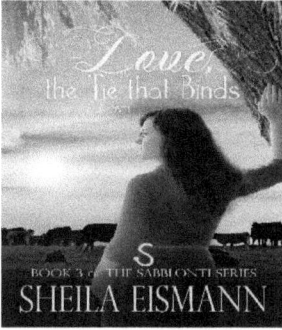

Desperation explodes when heiress Stormy Sabblonti Castins calculates her dwindling fortune in Book 3 of the Sabblonti Series, **Love the Tie that Binds.** Is she capable of learning the painful lessons of having to rely upon someone and something other than inherited wealth? As her husband, Chet, continues to heal from his near fatal accident, tormenting shadows of The Black Raven lurk in the background.

These high desert hills are alive with blessed babies, enchanting engagements, skillful scavengers, sophisticated scoundrels, rich revelations, timeless treasures, and western weddings.

The Main Sabblonti Ranch house abounds with an unexpected marriage, childrens' voices, and Sir Shelton sporting his silver bell.

In a captivating story of courage, trust, and faithfulness, will Stormy still be tied in knots or find lasting love by year's end?

Share the joys and sorrows of a mountain community in this swirling saga.

NOTES, REFLECTIONS, & THOUGHTS

NOTES, REFLECTIONS, &
THOUGHTS

NOTES, REFLECTIONS, & THOUGHTS

NOTES, REFLECTIONS, & THOUGHTS

Sheila Eismann

NOTES, REFLECTIONS, & THOUGHTS

NOTES, REFLECTIONS, & THOUGHTS